The 9 Types of Men
Women Will Encounter

Introducing The Equine Family

ORU AMADI

Copyright © 2023 Oru Amadi
All rights reserved.
ISBN: 9798395833495

DEDICATION

I dedicate this book to my family and friends. Some of whom are yet looking for that perfect mate. I also dedicate this book to my mother, Yvette Amadi, my grandmother, Carmalita "Pinks" Barriffe, and my father, Benjamin Amadi all of whom who has taught me many lessons in life and relationships.

ACKNOWLEDGMENTS

I am grateful for the support and inspiration of my sister Dene Brown, my fiancé Angie Rodriguez, my publisher Michelle P Crump, and all the individuals I have spoken with over the years about relationships. Without their encouragement and contribution, I wouldn't have been able to write this book and share this valuable knowledge with the world. Their kindness has truly been invaluable to me, and I am thankful for their help and support throughout this process. Thank you for allowing me into your lives and giving me the information needed to create this work.

Table of Content

Introduction 1

Chapter 1 – The Unicorn 3

Chapter 2 – The Stallion and Ascended Stallion 7

Chapter 3 – The Pony 15

Chapter 4 – The Working Category of Equine 19

    The Ascended Workhorse 20
    The Workhorse 24
    The Donkey 26

Chapter 5 – The Colt 29

Chapter 6 – The Dead Horse 33

Conclusion 37

A Mother's Love 39

About the Author 41

Introduction

Interpersonal relationships encompass the way individuals interact, form connections, and develop emotional, social, or romantic bonds. These connections can be within a family structure or beyond it. Communication is a critical component of any relationship, as it helps to build trust, resolve conflicts, and promote understanding. Trust is the foundation of healthy relationships, requiring confidence in the other person's reliability, integrity, and intentions. Respect is also essential, involving the valuing of each other's boundaries, opinions, and autonomy. To maintain healthy relationships, it is necessary to establish and respect personal boundaries, which define acceptable behavior, physical space, and emotional well-being. Mutual respect for each other's boundaries is crucial for fostering healthy relationships.

Building and maintaining relationships require a balance between connection and individuality. It's crucial for individuals to retain their sense of self while being together. This balance leads to a healthier and more sustainable relationships. Relationships can facilitate personal growth and development through shared experiences. It's essential to invest in respectful, positive, and mutually fulfilling connections. This book draws comparisons between certain categories of horses and men; however, it is important to remember that every man is different. So, whether you're a horse lover or not, the lessons in this book are applicable to everyone seeking a fulfilling relationship. I chose horses because my sister has loved them since she was young. I explained to her the different character traits of each type of horse and others in the equine family that are like some men.

She was able to pick up on the cues immediately. Just how you wouldn't choose a bloodhound to herd cattle or guard your flock, it's essential to select the right kind of man for your life. After speaking with and listening to hundreds of women over the years, I have compiled a list of men and their attributes. Let's dive in and explore each category to understand them better. However, if horses are not your thing, feel free to replace them with an animal that you can relate to. Choosing the right mate is crucial for our success and happiness. Certain breeds of animals cannot exist or live together, and the same rules may apply to humans. For instance, if you are a couch potato who doesn't like going for walks, you may not want to choose a high-octane whippet or Dalmatian as a pet dog. This book is written from most desired men, as stated by women to the least.

Chapter One

The Unicorn

The man of every woman's dreams.

I once helped my mother find a suitable companion, as she had a history of choosing the wrong type of men. Being in her sixties, I wanted to make sure she found someone who was a good match for her. I asked her to describe the kind of man she was looking for. I was taken back by the list of requirements she shared with me. Most of them were the sort of things you'd expect to hear from someone much younger. She insisted that he had to be wealthy and have at least two million in the bank. She even suggested that he should give her half of his fortune. I gently explained to her that finding a man like that was like finding a unicorn or a needle in a haystack as they're extremely rare, and not something that you can simply wait for. You must actively seek them out, just like a treasure hunter or gold digger.

Kicking things off is our Unicorn! This type of man tops the list of 99.9% of women, no matter what the age. These men have an overabundance of things a women wants or desire in a mate. They are financially, materially, physically, mentally, sexually, emotionally, and socially affluent, but most importantly they are willing to get on their knees or bend over backward for their woman. They require nothing of her in return. She can look and act any way she wants or do anything she wants. This man will be right there to the ends of time despite any baggage or drama she may bring along with her. He will have a chiseled smile and a grateful heart through it all. His sole purpose in life is to serve his queen and make her happy.

Finding the ideal man can sometimes feel like searching for a unicorn. Many women spend a significant portion, if not all, of their lives seeking this type of man, only to come up empty-handed. This is because this type of man is often portrayed in movies, novels, and legends, much like the mythical creatures. However, just like unicorns, there have been accounts of real-life sightings, and with the vastness of the world, it is possible that this man exists somewhere, waiting for his queen to find him. It is important to note that it is up to you to find him, and not wait for him to find you. One common misconception is that rare and valuable things will come looking for us, but when has that ever happened? Just like treasure hunters, oil, or gold diggers, or those seeking a unicorn, you must put in the work and search for what you desire. So, if you truly believe in unicorns and you have the time, resources and fortitude go out there, embark on your quest, and find your ideal partner - your unicorn. This man is for those women who believe there is magic in the world. They are willing to chance never having a relationship, for that one in a million shot, that they will find him. It doesn't matter the character or the looks, this man will sweep you up in his arms and whisk you away.

The 9 Types of Men Women Will Encounter

The Unicorn

Chapter Two

The Stallion and Ascended Stallion

The man that stands out of the crowd.

As time passes, some women start to believe that finding the "unicorn" man is a difficult task. They realize that they need to put aside their unrealistic expectations from movies and books and take a realistic approach. Still, they look for what they consider as the next best thing, which is the "Stallion Man." If you've ever watched a herd of horses, you know there's always one that stands out from the rest. Similarly, in the world of men, there are two types of Stallions: the ascended Stallion and the Stallion. From a young age, boys may notice that certain other boys are receiving attention from girls. These boys are often deemed cute and receive special treatment such as snacks and birthday party invitations. This phenomenon is also seen in media and celebrity culture.

As they enter puberty, boys may feel pressured to gain attention from girls, even if they do not have traditionally attractive looks. They may observe that boys who appear similar to them but have more expensive clothing or come from wealthier backgrounds seem to attract girls. This can lead to a desire to acquire money by any means necessary in order to become more competitive in the dating game. As a man grows older, it seems that he needs to make more money to attract females. In middle school, he could simply wear name brand clothes and buy girls ice cream or candy. In high school, he needs to have name brand clothes, an expensive cellphones, jewelry, a new or expensive car, and money to take her on dates. As a young adult between the ages of eighteen to twenty-four he must have all the previously mentioned things.

In addition to that, his own apartment, shopping sprees for her, travel, and pay for both his and her bills. However, this reality only works successfully for a young man in that age group if he comes from money, make it in the entertainment industry, landed a high-paying job, or started a business. Once these young men have attained financial success, the world of women opens to them. Living the life of a Stallion is not easy. You must constantly pay to stay in the spotlight and compete with other Stallions who are also trying to take over. When your Lamborghini or private jet starts showing signs of wear and tear, you must prepare to spend hundreds of thousands, if not millions, to replace it. Moreover, you must deal with a constant stream of women who are only interested in your money, and not forming a real relationship with you. This is why most men give up on the Stallion life after they turn around age twenty-six. Those who can afford to stay in demand only settle for the best. When I was in my late twenties, I had a taste of the Stallion life, but I wasn't an actual Stallion. Although I had a great body from working out, my possessions didn't scream wealth and attention.

Although I didn't have millions of dollars, I was grateful to have a decent job that covered all my expenses and a business that added to my savings. My home was not a mansion, but a comfortable 4-bedroom split foyer. My vehicles were not expensive or brand-new, but they were both paid off and reliable. Despite not having a lavish lifestyle, I was doing well compared to many men my age. I had no trouble attracting women. One day, I met a woman who caught my eye, and we started dating. On our first date, she shared that she recently lost her job, car, and home, and was currently living with her parents and her daughter. Despite her circumstances, I was drawn to her kind personality and decided to continue seeing her. As we got to know each other better, we discussed the qualities we looked for in a partner.

One day I asked her to cook for me just to see if she was invested in what we were building, but she refused. Her reasoning was that she would not do this until we were officially in a relationship. This didn't make sense to me, as she already knew who I was, and what I could, and was offering. It seemed as if she expected me to take a risk on her and commit without knowing if she was truly what she claimed to be. And why would I take that risk when I had multiple women to choose from? Women who were willing to do upfront, what she refused to do? So, I didn't see the point in taking the risk. However, my now fiancé was different. She showed me without reservations, what she was willing to do to secure a relationship with me. If I had these types of options available to me when I wasn't even putting on a show of wealth or status, imagine what's available to the actual "Stallion Men" that do put on a show and what their expectations and demands are.

The 9 Types of Men Women Will Encounter

The Ascended Stallion

The Ascended Stallion

The man that has it all and is looking to share it with that one special woman.

This is the type of man who seems to have it all. Women are drawn to him like moths to a flame. He exudes confidence and charm, and he has all the trappings of success - money, status, and material possessions. It's as if he's a rare breed of horse, with impeccable looks and an undeniable presence. And yet, despite the attention he receives, this man is known for having a heart of gold. He's not interested in a revolving door of relationships; he's looking for a life partner. When he finds her, he is committed to making her his own. Once he's off the market, he's either quickly married or remains single for life, which makes him similar to a unicorn.

These Types of men are usually white-collar CEO's, inventors, in some type of medical profession, politicians, older ex-athletes, entertainers, attorneys, etc. I've been asked by many women where do they find these men. These men are usually at their place of business, at a high-end restaurants or events, such as museums, wine tastings, or a high-end fundraisers. They prefer the front-row seat of events, which is very expensive such as sports, games, etc. If they are not married or seriously dating, they are alone, or in the company of Stallions. The ascended Stallion is the one that women desire the most, as he embodies qualities such as strength, dominance, and success. This man is best for women who desire the finer things in life, money, trips, luxury cars and status. However, they must be rated eight (8) and up by STRANGERS on looks and eight (8) and up on character. And they must be willing to compete against hundreds of women until marriage.

The 9 Types of Men Women Will Encounter

The Stallion

Stands out amongst the herd.

The Stallion is that man that has it all and is eager to show it off to many women.

This individual embodies the traits of the Ascended Stallion, but with one significant difference. They prioritize having fun, enjoying the company of multiple partners, and relishing the attention that comes with their status. Being financially well-off means that they have the freedom to do as they please, and women flock to them on their terms. Their goal in life is to live it to the fullest and showcase their wealth and success to the world. They only consider settling down once they have outgrown the Stallion lifestyle, passing the torch down to their younger successors. Typically, these Stallions are athletes, entertainers, investors, or are engaged in some type of illegal activities. Like their ascended counterparts, they can be found anywhere that allows them to flaunt their status as a Stallion.

It's important for women to understand that even when they are in a committed relationship, there are still many other women who are actively pursuing the same men. Therefore, it's crucial to always be aware and vigilant, as there will be others who are willing to do things that you wouldn't do to take your place. Additionally, if you're one of the many women who are picky and passing up on good men, you may end up waiting in line for years, only to be rejected in a matter of seconds when your turn finally comes. This man is for women who are willing to share their man for the finer things in life compiled with fame and staying in the limelight. If all you have going for you is your looks, then THIS is your man. You must be rated at least an eight (8) or higher in looks. If you can fake a decent character when you are around him, your personality doesn't matter.

Chapter Three

The Pony

The man that uses his looks and sex as money.

I have a female family member that has a successful career. She is beautiful, and in her twenties. It seems as if she has everything going for her except her taste in men. I noticed that she always choses men that she believes looks great but have absolutely nothing going for them. Because of this, she always ends up taking care of them financially. I could never understand why she settles for these types of men when there are so many better choices out there. Each time the relationships followed the same path. Mind-blowing passion, and awesome vacations, but all on her dime. The love just seems to never stop bubbling and blossoming, to the point that they would want to move in with her, which she gladly accepts.

Then three to four months later, it ends with the male moving on to another woman. That other woman is always in the same or higher pay grade. After getting impregnated twice by the same type of male, even marrying one of them, I had to sit her down to get to the bottom of the dysfunction. I wanted to know why she continues to choose these types of males. After asking her some hard-hitting questions, I realized that she wasn't going out of her way to choose these types of males, but in fact, they were targeting her! I discovered that it was not just her, but women that were to be considered as the modern career woman. It was apparent to me that these males were strategic in their approach. They positioned themselves to always be where the modern woman would be, such as her job, or on vacation.

And because they are on a mission, they are willing to do and be whatever it takes to disarm, their already, distracted prey. Once they spot their target, they go in for the kill, sinking their teeth in deep. And that's when I introduced my female family member to the Pony. Many people may wonder why this man is so sought after by women. However, the answer is quite simple. This type of man is always there for you when you need him. For women who have spent years trying to win over the first few guys on the list, only to find themselves competing with countless other women, this man is a breath of fresh air. He comes to you, rather than making you wait in line. And while he may not have the same status or wealth as the first two types of men, he has a certain charm and confidence that is hard to resist. It's easy to overlook his lack of ambition or financial stability when you're caught up in the moment, and that's exactly what makes him so dangerous. His good looks and smooth talking are nothing more than a ploy to get you in bed, and many women fall for it time and time again. So be careful who you give your heart to, because not all men are who they seem to be. It's no secret that some men seem to have a way with words. They'll charm you with their sweet talk and make you believe in their dreams of starting a business or changing careers. But don't be fooled by their smooth words.

Once they've moved in with you, you'll soon find out that they were fired from their last job and expect you to support them until they find new work. Weeks turn into months, and months turn into years, as they take advantage of your generosity and refuse to take responsibility for their own lives. These men are like ponies - cute and pretty to look at, but ultimately useless. They have no real ambition or drive. They will stay in your bed and house if you're willing to foot the bill. They may work blue-collar jobs or hang out where successful career women congregate, hoping to find someone to take care of them. But don't be fooled – they probably won't change, and you can't make them grow up. The pony is an animal that only grows to a certain size then stops. Ponies are made for little girl, they are cute, sweet and make wonderful pet, and draw a lot of attention from onlookers.

So be careful who you let into your life, because not all men are worth your time and energy. It's important to be aware of these men that hide within jobs such as janitors, cooks, bartenders, and personal trainers, who tend to frequently switch jobs or have significant gaps in their employment history. These individuals are often seen as a fallback option for modern or working women, who they know will support them financially. They will do whatever it takes to keep the money flowing, including becoming whoever their partner wants them to be, and may even go as far as getting married and having children. It's crucial to understand that these individuals see themselves as ponies and are willing to have multiple owners. So, even if you are married to them, it's likely that you will be sharing them with other women. Be cautious of who you let into your life. These type of men can waste your time and energy. You don't have to worry about searching for this man, if you have money, he will find you. This man is for women who are affluent, career driven, and don't like to be under the leadership of a man. If you like to boast that "you are a strong independent woman and don't need no man", view men as accessories, or treat them like the "maintenance" man, he will fit right in line with your life. However, It's IMPERATIVE to remember you must keep that same energy throughout your entire relationship. If not, he will move on to the next, wealthier woman. Your looks or character aren't that important, all that matters is your money and your ability to provide the lifestyle he wants. But understand that if you are a masculine woman, and not very attractive, he will more likely have a few attractive, feminine women on the side. Keep in mind his entertainment will be at your expense because it will be your money he's doing it with.

The 9 Types of Men Women Will Encounter

The Pony

Chapter Four

The Working Category of Equine

It's frustrating to see how the media constantly focuses on the same few men and portrays them as the epitome of masculinity. It's as if society has decided that only those who have wealth, status, and good looks are worthy of attention and admiration. However, this narrow definition of masculinity ignores the fact that there are many other types of men who exist and contribute to society in their own way. It's unfortunate that these men are often overlooked and forgotten, only coming into the spotlight briefly when something needs to be fixed or put right. But even then, they quickly fade away and return to the shadows. It's time for society to recognize and celebrate all types of men, not just the ones who fit a certain mold.

It's interesting how the horse world is similar to society in some ways. All the attention and admiration are given to the Stallion and even the ponies, while the hardworking horses who are the backbone of the entire equine ecosystem are often overlooked. Very few people look beyond the golden fields and notice the horse laden with straps and till, pulling the tiller to build and sow a new field for all the horses to eat and live, or the horse pulling the feed wagon to feed everyone. To the majority, this horse is just a basic dirty workhorse, not realizing its importance. In men, we have three types of workhorses - the Ascended Workhorse, the Regular Workhorse, and the Donkey.

The 9 Types of Men Women Will Encounter

The Ascended Workhorse

The man that works hard for his money, but rarely flaunts it.

It's interesting to note that there are different types of men in society, just like how there are different types of horses in the equine world.

There are some men who are like undercover stallions or stallions on a budget. They don't flaunt their wealth or status like the typical stallion, but when they do come out of hiding, they can be mistaken for one. These men are hardworking and tend to be more frugal with their money, but they still enjoy the finer things in life. You won't see them cruising around in luxury cars every day, but you might spot them in a decked-out pickup truck or SUV that can also be used for work. They may not have the 6 pack abs and dashing looks you will find in a Stallion. However, you may occasionally see a Benz parked on their ranch or their custom-built house, which they use to show off when they feel like it.

These men are usually the owners of small businesses who work alongside the people they employ or high-level blue-collar workers who supervise. They tend to be understated and practical, and their work attire may not necessarily turn heads. However, as soon as they clean up, the women come flocking, only to be reminded that he isn't a full stallion, and will eventually put back on his halter, and working shoes to head back to work. Some women believe that they can push him to become a full stallion and attain the lifestyle and attention that comes with it, but they fail to realize that it comes with everything else that being a stallion entails. It's funny, as I write this, I think back on a relationship I had in my late twenties. I had come to the realization around the age of twenty-five, maybe twenty-six, that I didn't want or need to be a stallion.

I had settled into my workhorse ways and was working on my ascension. I was into internet dating back then and met a lady online. Through conversations, she told me she was an attorney and the type of lifestyle she lived. Immediately I knew that we would not be a good fit, as I could tell she was materialistically minded. In addition to that, she lived over an hour away from me. But she insisted we meet me in person. She said she was willing to make that drive herself as she loved to drive. So, I conceded. We decided a mall would be our meetup place. I was dressed casual and basic, but she came through all dolled up. Everything she had on was brand name. I was sporting my Walmart and probably some Goodwill gear, if I remember correctly. So, at one point I pulled out my Nokia to check a message, and the horror that came into her eyes almost made me jump! She couldn't believe I had such an old basic phone. Immediately she started telling me how I had to get a new phone. I kindly told her that I was quite happy with my Nokia, and it did everything I needed it to do. Fast forward to the end of our meetup, she wanted us to continue seeing each other, despite the distance, and us being complete opposites.

Now that I think of it, it's possible she thought of me as a pony, as this was back in my gym rat days. I didn't have the money of a stallion, but I was built as one. She was attractive and had an interesting personality, so we continued our courtship. As I walked her to her vehicle, to my surprise, we were parked in the same isle. I pointed to my truck to let her know where I was parked. Again, the horror in her eyes would mimic those on the run in a horror movie. Immediately, she said I needed to get a new vehicle because my truck was too old. She also stated that her brother could get me a great deal. I calmly explained to her that I was very happy with my completely paid off 98 Dodge Dakota, and I would be driving it until the wheels fall off.

After our conversation, I realized it would not work out, so I told her it would be wise for us to go our separate ways, because it was obvious that we were too different. Again, she insisted that she wanted us to continue. Moving things along, during our very short six months relationship, she tried numerous times to turn me into something I was not. Her dreams were for us to become, and I quote "Socialites of Atlanta" but in that same breath, she was insecure of every woman that came within 50 ft of me. I asked her, If she was already suspicious about me, and other women, what did she think would happen if I started flaunting my wealth or behaving like a stallion? Unfortunately, she was never able to comprehend this, which only fueled her anxiety, pushing our relationship to its end.

This man is for women who enjoys the finer things in life but doesn't care to be in the limelight, but still adheres to traditional values and mindset. You also must be willing to compete with many women until he picks you. Your looks can be rated a six and up and your character or personality an eight and up.

The 9 Types of Men Women Will Encounter

The Workhorse

The understated common man who powers the world

This type of man is usually passed up by 70% of women because he just doesn't shine like the first five do. Like his equine counterparts, he is just a basic horse working the back fields. He's usually living in a basic house, driving a basic car, working your basic job or business. His clothes are basic and probably always dirty if he works a dirty job, even his words are basic instead of those words of honey women look for in the past five men. This man is just straight to the point. As mentioned earlier 70% or more of women will turn their nose up at this basic man and continue their chase of the first five. However, just like the few that noticed the workhorse working the back fields, the observant women will take a pause and notice something, which is the workhorse, in all his basicness is the backbone of the equine world.

He's the one that powers the entire system, and without him, nothing would function as it should, especially all the things she enjoys. Even the Stallion calls on the workhorse to handle things his show muscles can't, which is why you'll often find workhorse and stallion rivalries. As she continues to watch him, she notices what happens when he unveils his identity. Once his saddle, reins, and halter come off and he washes all the dirt and grime off him, there is literally a Stallion standing in front of her, with huge rippling work muscles. But he quickly gets dressed because he doesn't care for all the attention the Stallion lives for. He purposely lives within or below his means so he can enjoy the simple pleasures of life and handle his responsibilities.

The workhorse is the backbone that powers the entire system. Even though most women overlook them because they are considered basic. However, they possess stability and core values that are fundamental to their character. They value traditional women who bring positivity and peace to their lives, and they have no tolerance for anyone who disrupts their peace. These men are often found working as hourly blue-collar jobs and trade workers. You can spot them at hole in the wall bars, grocery stores, libraries, and hardware stores. Unlike the Stallion who has women shopping for them, they shop for themselves. They prioritize their responsibilities and take pleasure in the simple things in life, unlike the stallion who seeks attention. This man is for women who are traditional and seek stability and dependability in their lives. While they like nice things, they are equally happy with a plain but comfortable lifestyle. Home bodies do well with this type of man.

The Donkey

The man that is a powerhouse but is overlooked because of society standards.

At first glance, people may not only laugh but judge a donkey based on its appearance and rumors about them. However, those who are knowledgeable understand that donkeys are much more than what meets the eye. Despite being known for their stubbornness, donkeys are incredibly loyal and strong creatures. They are miniature workhorses that can reach places, pulling and packing loads that regular workhorses cannot. They are also used as protectors of livestock. Similarly, there are men who are often dismissed by women due to physical, mental, or social ailments beyond their control. These men may be short, physically unattractive, stutter, have anxiety or be socially and sexually awkward.

But just like donkeys, if the right person comes along and shows them love and appreciation, they will do everything in their power to make their partner satisfied and happy. These men can be found where you find workhorses. They are usually put in the friendzone by women because they can carry their weight and emotional baggage, similar to donkeys. These issues are usually brought on by dealing with other men. They are more patient, understanding, and willing to deal with women that other men won't. Unfortunately, because of this, many of these men are your "nice guys" and may even simp for women to rescue them or get their attention. However, those who mistreat them will quickly learn that they are not to be underestimated, and they will move on to someone who appreciates them for who they are.

It's also important to understand that just because a man is short doesn't immediately make him a donkey. A short man with money, makes him as tall as a stallion. If you need to be constantly held up, and reassured in life, this man is for you. He will also provide you with the lifestyle you want if it's within his means. You must remember, just like an actual donkey, you can't overburden him. He can only take so much, so be prepared to take off some of the load, if you see he's overwhelmed. On looks you can be rated 4 and up and your character the same.

The 9 Types of Men Women Will Encounter

The Donkey

Chapter Five

The Colt

The man that's depending on you to grow.

I believe in helping those who are less fortunate. I have provided job opportunities to many individuals who are experiencing difficult times.

Through work, I have encountered men in various stages of life who had different reasons for starting over. Some of these men have taken my help and have successfully turned their lives around, thanking me for giving them a chance, when no one else did. However, there have been some who, despite being given all the necessary tools to change their lives, have not put in the effort required, and have expected me to take care of them. Which brings me to the next member of the equine family, The Colt. The colt is a baby horse. When we think of a baby, we think of defenseless, vulnerable, and needy.

A baby is a being who is fully dependent on their mother to grow, just as some men. I personally believe men at this stage of their lives need to be left on their own to figure things out as a man. Many times, women come in, thinking they are helping, but in reality, do more damage than good. When a man is at the bottom and gets up on his own feet, there is pride, and power in that. One day I saw a homeless man lying on the street. I went over to talk to him because I needed help for a business I was planning on starting. I asked him if he would like an opportunity to get off the streets and change his life.

He told me he had a drug problem, in which I replied, if he was willing to go to AA classes, and not abuse drugs anymore, I would be willing to work with him. But he had to be willing to make a change. I brought him to my property, provided a place for him to sleep, and gave him some new clothes. I even penned out a life plan with him. I saw genuine excitement in his eyes, especially when I mentioned saving up to get his own house in a year. Not only did this guy do great work for me, but he also gave me 95% of his paycheck to put away in savings. He was afraid that if he had easy access to his money, he would waist it all it. I reconnected him with his mother and signed him up for AA classes. We had a great working relationship, until his old girlfriend came in the picture. He wanted to know if she could move in with him because she was in a shelter. I really did not want it to happen, but he said he was lonely he was tired being by himself. Shortly after he started complaining about working and no social life. We were geographically in an area where nothing much exciting happened, so I empathized with him.

He also stated that her being there would be an advantage because she would take care of the domestic duties and get a job at a restaurant down the street. They also discussed saving together for their new home. It was clear to me that his mind was already made up. In addition, he was convinced that she was a great role model and would be a great influence in his life, especially with his recovery. I figured the man had been doing such a great job, that I should give him this as an encouragement to keep on the right path. Well, within two hours of me allowing this woman to move onto my property, the man was asking me for some of his savings. Now, since he started working for me, he never asked me to give him money. I was curious that he did, so, I asked him why. His response was "oh! I haven't been able to do anything for my girlfriend in a while. I want to buy her something nice."

I told him that was nice of him but reminded him of our goals. However, at the end of the day, it was his money, so I gave him the amount he asked for. It was only three days after, the man came back for another withdrawal. I got so tired of constantly having to make bank trips for him, that I finally withdrew all his money and gave it to him. In less than two weeks, the man was completely broke and asking me for loans. In less than three months, I severed ties with him. I could no longer depend on him to show up for work because he was tending to her needs, or should I say, issues. This was a classic example of a man that was on a mission to better himself, and was doing well, until he allowed a woman to come in and distract him from his goals.

Which is why I must reiterate that most times these men need to figure their lives out on their own. Even with this true life-story, there are women today that feels as if they can be the exception. Although nothing in life is absolute, just understand the time and resources you will be investing. There is no way of knowing what end you will end up with. It's not uncommon to come across men who are actively working to improve their lives to join the ranks of successful individuals. These men are often young and trying to find their place in the world. Many of them have been through difficult times and are working hard in trying to turn things around. Some may have a troubled past, but they are determined to change, and become productive members of society. While these men have a lot of potential, they may need patience and support, as they navigate the obstacles of life.

It's hard to predict what their future holds, but one thing is for sure - they will always appreciate those who help them along the way. Even if they go on to achieve great things. They will never forget those who believed in them and offered a helping hand. These type of men are for women who like to try and build a man. Women that take chances and love to gamble. You must have time, patience, and some resources. You must also be prepared to walk away from the table losing everything you put down. Your looks and character don't matter, as the colt will latch on to anyone who is willing to rear him into independence. However, once he is fully grown, he calls the shots, as he will let you know exactly which way he will decide to go. But during his growth and development, you will see signs, that will tell you which equine he will most likely grow into.

The 9 Types of Men Women Will Encounter

The Colt

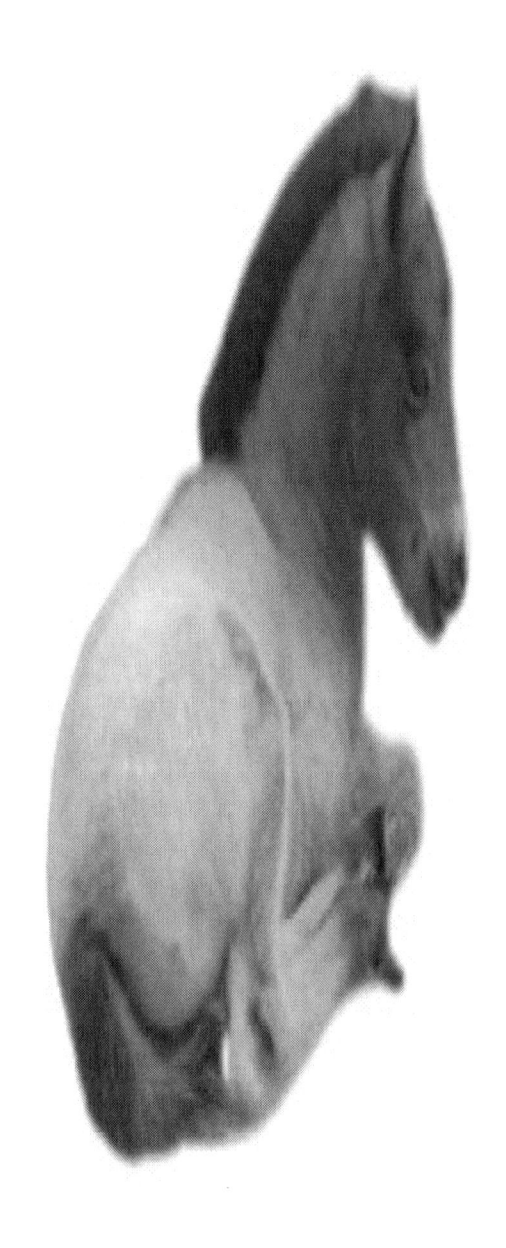

Chapter Six

The Dead Horse

The man with no future.

I remember encountering a homeless couple who were living in their car. As a compassionate person, I decided to let them camp on my property. At first, I thought they were working diligently to save up money and get back on their feet. However, as time went on, I began to realize that only the woman was working. I assumed that the man had a disability that prevented him from contributing to their situation. One day, he offered to do some work for me around my property. I agreed to pay him for his work and instructed him to contact me once the job was completed. Unfortunately, I didn't hear from him for two days. Eventually, I received a text from his lady friend asking me for a loan.

I was confused because I knew I had given the man a job that paid five times what she was asking for. He was supposed to have finished the job two days prior and contact me so that I could inspect it. When I asked her about the job, she said she wasn't informed about it. So, I decided to stop in to see how the work was coming along. When I arrived, I found that nothing had been done, and the person in charge was knocked out, high on drugs. When I woke him up, he gave me a ridiculous excuse for why the job was not done. Over the months of getting to know the couple, the lady revealed to me the reason she kept asking for a loan. She explained that her male friend was addicted to drugs, and he smoked away all their bill money. I decided to help by offering him work so he could buy necessities for himself and her.

However, he always had excuses for why he couldn't work, leaving the woman drowning and struggling without any means of support. I encountered this type of man for the first time, and I cannot call him a pony because a pony takes care of himself and seeks high-class living and women to support them. This man, however, is the dead horse- emotionally, mentally, and physically unavailable. He was contented with his lifestyle, living in squalor. He consumed so many drugs that he resembled a skeleton. These men possess many traits that's in the pony, they just don't have the looks. They are habitual addicts and criminals that have absolutely no interest in bettering their lives. They are physically unattractive and do not care about their appearance. This man is for woman who have nothing going for themselves or the new age feminist. If all you have to offer is sex and you just want a body to be next to, then this is your man. Looks and character won't matter as he will be too high or detached from reality to care or notice. They refuse help from everyone, including their loved ones. They are not looking for a hand-up but a handout. These men are usually homeless with a fully functioning mind, living in their parent's basements, shelters, or on a friend's couch. They have no interest in changing their situation.

Trying to do anything with them is a complete waste of time and energy. And that concludes the nine types of men women will encounter in this world. While these are important evaluations, it's crucial that you take your time to truly get to know your potential partner. Remember, this is simply a starting point for your journey into the world of men. It's no use finding an ascended stallion or workhorse if they turn out to be abusive, deceitful, or lacking in respect for good women. Only the unicorn will possess everything you're looking for, though we all know how rare they are.

The 9 Types of Men Women Will Encounter

The Dead Horse

Conclusion

In concluding you are probably wondering or is curious to know where I would place myself in these categories of this book, The Nine Types of Men Women Will Encounter, Introducing The Equine Family. It can be very difficult to subject myself to self-evaluation because it is often limited in perspective. Nevertheless, those who know me well have identified me as a workhorse, and I agree. I may also have a slight inclination towards ascension, but material possessions and attention-seeking are not priorities for me. During a conversation with a friend who shares some of the same work ethics I have, I asked how much income would make him feel successful in life and how would he spend it.

He gave me a specific amount and then planned to move to South Beach, Florida and purchase a mansion on the beach. I was confused, so I asked why he would want to be amidst the chaos. He explained that he enjoys the beach and feels safer surrounded by people of similar wealth. I understood his words, but the truth is that there are many peaceful and relatively quiet beaches in Florida where one can live safely. So, the real reason he wanted to live in South Beach was for the status it provided. He liked the attention he got when driving his Maybach down the street. He asked me the same question, and I responded that I too wanted a mansion, but in a secluded area with a ranch where only my close family and friends knew its location.

When I go into town, my vehicle blends in with everyone else's. He laughed and called me crazy, but it showed that deep down, he also desires to be a stallion. His business just hasn't taken him there yet. It's important to remember that while these are essential factors, the character of a person will always be the most critical aspect to consider. It's imperative to take time to get to know your potential partner. For example, my friend may seem like an ordinary workhorse, but asking simple questions revealed that money is the only thing stopping him from achieving more success. Always keep in mind that a person's true character can be revealed by the more money they come into. To truly understand someone's mind and heart, don't be afraid to ask deep questions, even those that seem theoretical or unrealistic.

However, this is just the beginning of your journey into the world of relationships. It's important to avoid choosing a partner who may have negative qualities such as being abusive, dishonest, or lacking respect for women. The ideal partner, like a unicorn will possess all the qualities you desire, but they may be difficult to find. However, if you want something bad enough you will seek it with your whole heart. Thank you for purchasing this book, and may you find your soulmate with the help of these insights.

A Mother's Love

A Tribute To My Mother

I consider myself a quiet, yet resourceful person, who tends to blend in rather than stand out. I possess many of my mother's qualities, including being strong, quiet, and assertive. My mother worked hard throughout her life, and I admire and emulate that quality. I know what I want and am willing to work hard to achieve it. When I was younger, I felt a strong desire to help the homeless, which I now realize is one of my mother's traits. She would often give her own clothes to those in need. Once, I gave her my favorite hoodie because she was cold. She looked so happy and comfortable wearing it. Later, when I asked where it was, she told me she had given it to a homeless man she met while doing community outreach work.

I loved that hoodie but was so proud of my mom for making a difference in someone's life. My mother was an incredible woman who touched the lives of people from all walks of life. It didn't matter their nationality, age, gender, or economic status. I believe success for her was making an impact and influence in everyone she encountered. No matter how successful she became she never forgot where she came from. She was always willing to reach back to help those less fortunate. She taught me that success is not always measured by material possessions, but rather by personal fulfillment and happiness. My mother was a devote Christian that taught her children the importance of prayer and having a personal relationship with God. While I miss her dearly I take comfort in knowing that she is in the arms of her heavenly father.

The 9 Types of Men Women Will Encounter

Dorethyvette Amadi

1959-2022

About The Author
Oru Amadi

Oru Amadi is a unique individual with a Jamaican mother and a Nigerian father, born in Milwaukee, Wisconsin. Despite having humble beginnings, he spent his early years in Jamaica with his grandparents, who instilled in him a love for farming and animals. During this time, he studied the nature of animals as it relates to humans. After returning to America with his mother and settling in Stone Mountain, GA, he attended and completed high school. Later in life, Oru embarked on a journey to visit other states and meet people from various cultures and nationalities, which became one of the highlights of his travels. During his travels, he interviewed men and women of all ages and backgrounds on the topic of relationships, which became the foundation of his first book, *"The 9 Types of Men Women Will Encounter."* Today, Oru is a real estate investor and an entrepreneur based in Snellville, GA, where he manages his businesses and enjoys life with the people close to his heart.

The Author's Information
Oru Amadi
Email: O1Amadi@hotmail.com

Thank you for purchasing this book.

Publisher's Information
MPC Creative Publishing & Designs LLC
Email: mpccreativepublishing@gmail.com
Ph: 954-479-2563

Made in the USA
Columbia, SC
20 July 2023